Terry Denton
Ted Greenwood
Paul Jennings

SPiT it OuT!

Illustrated by
Terry Denton

A Puffin Book

Puffin Books

Published by the Penguin Group
Penguin Books Australia
250 Camberwell Road
Camberwell, Victoria 3124, Australia
Penguin Books Ltd
80 Strand, London WC2R ORL, England
Penguin Putnam Inc.
375 Hudson Street, New York, New York 10014, USA
Penguin Books, a division of Pearson Canada
10 Alcorn Avenue, Toronto, Ontario, Canada, M4V 3B2
Penguin Books (N.Z.) Ltd
Cnr Rosedale and Airborne Roads, Albany, Auckland, New Zealand
Penguin Books (South Africa) (Pty) Ltd
24 Sturdee Avenue, Rosebank, Johannesburg 2196, South Africa
Penguin Books India (P) Ltd
11, Community Centre, Panchsheel Park, New Delhi, 110 017, India

First published by Penguin Books Australia, 2003

10 9 8 7 6 5 4 3 2 1

Cover and text design by George Dale
Printed and bound in Australia by McPherson's Printing Group, Maryborough, Victoria

National Library of Australia
Cataloguing-in-Publication data:

Denton, Terry, 1950- .
Spit it out!

For children.
ISBN 0 14 330041 5.
1. Play on words - Juvenile literature. I. Jennings, Paul,
1943- . II. Greenwood, Ted, 1930-1999. III. Title.

A820.8

www.puffin.com.au

For
Ted Greenwood
P. J. & T.D.

This book is chockers
with Katt and Ratt stuff,
and there are jokes
and riddles all over
the place

Contents

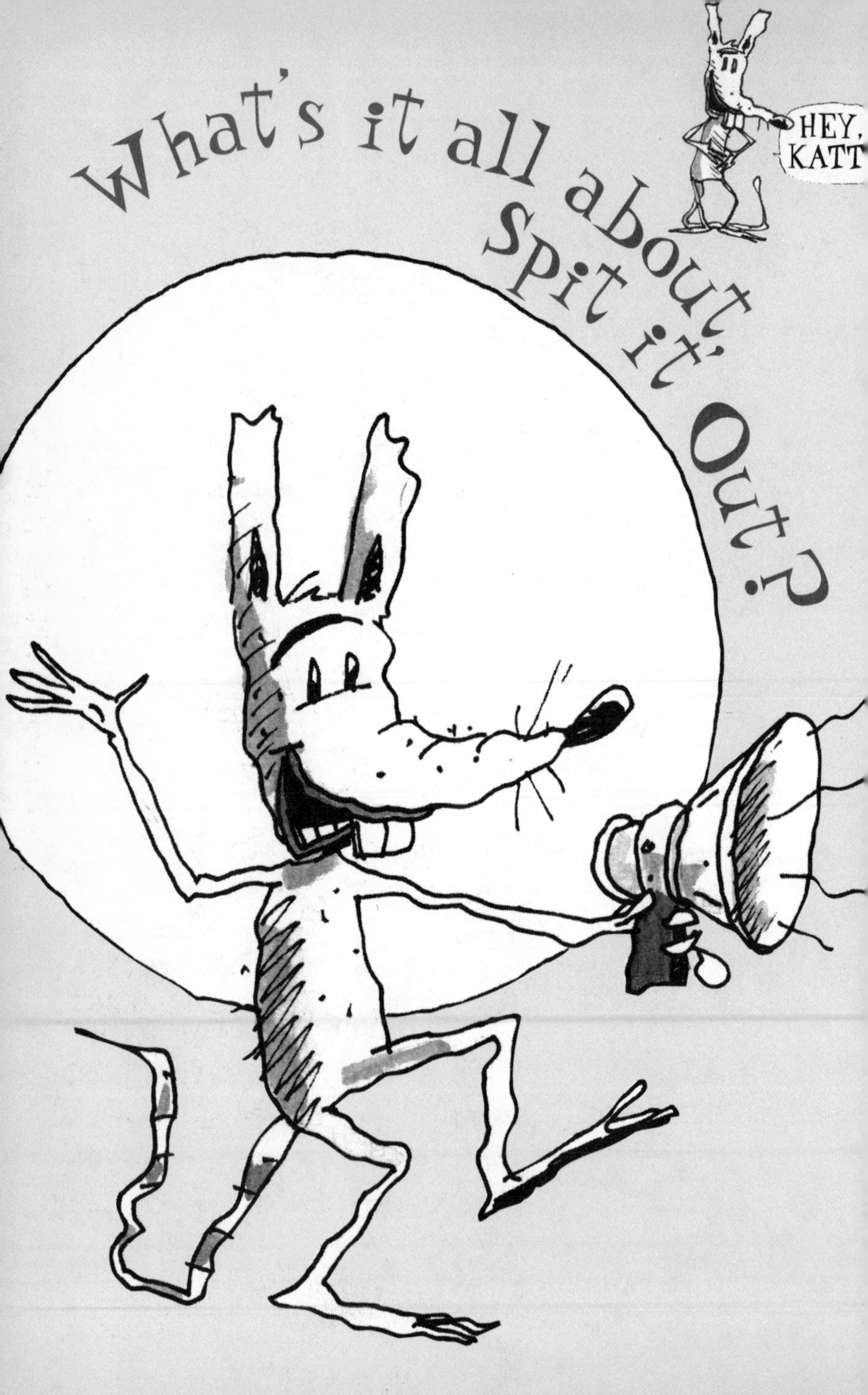
What's it all about, Spit it Out?
HEY, KATT

Pirates are a rum lot, Ratty!

Not all of them, Katt, some are teatotallers!

Jokes & riddles to rattle your brain box*

Katt and Ratt tell a few . . . .

*And improve your IQ.

Start laughing!

Q: WHERE DO YOU BUY RUDE T-SHIRTS?

A: THE MEN'S SWEAR DEPARTMENT.

SILLY ★🎯回!!* HERE

Q: Why do cats always lose at cards?

A: Because they get paw hands.

YIPEEE!

Q: WHICH ATHLETES ARE THE COLDEST?

A: POLE VAULTERS.

Q: Why do shepherds make good prisoners?

A: They're used to being behind baas.

BAAA BAAA BAAA

Q: WHAT DO YOU GET WHEN YOU CROSS A BOTTLE OF GLUE WITH AN EMU?

A: A STICKY BEAK.

Q: HOW DO YOU KNOW IF THERE ARE DUCKS IN YOUR ROOF?

A: QUACKS IN THE CEILING.

Q: What do you call a lamb dressed in underwear?

A: Bra bra black sheep.

Q: WHY CAN'T THE THREE BEARS GO TO BED?

A: BECAUSE GOLDIE LOCKS THEM OUT.

Q: How did the cowboy talk to his pony?

A: In a hoarse voice.

Q: WHAT DID THE PRIEST SAY WHEN HE SAW MOSQUITOES IN THE CHURCH?

A: LET US SPRAY!

Q: Why did the elephant put clothes up his nose?

A: He was told to pack his trunk.

Q: WHAT DO YOU CALL A SMELLY SANTA?

A: FARTER CHRISTMAS.

Q: Which cat has pimples on his feet?

A: Pus in boots.

Q: What exercise do cats like?

A: Puss ups.

Q: What do you call a rooster on a toilet?

A: Cock-a-doodle-loo.

Q: Why did the
musician laugh?

A: He was playing
a joke.

Q: WHY DON'T YOU TELL
SECRETS TO A CLOCK?

A: BECAUSE TIME
WILL TELL.

Q: Why wouldn't
Goldilocks go into
the fruit shop?

A: Because of the
three pears.

Q: What do you call
twin roosters?

A: Cock-a-doodle two.

Q: Why don't bulls make good salesmen?

A: They charge too much.

Q: What does a koala eat when it's stuck up a tree?

A: Chewing gum.

Q: WHAT DO YOU CALL A BACON HAMBURGER?

A: A PIG MAC.

Q: Why should you bury a greengrocer in a vegetable patch?

A: So he can rest in peas.

SNUFFLE

Q: WHAT DO GET IF YOU PUT PEPPER ON A HANDKERCHIEF?

A: A TISSUE.

Q: What do you call a rooster's ghost?

A: Cock-a-doodle-boo!

BOoooooooo.!!

Let's move on ...

to picture riddles

Each **CLUE** has a letter and number beside it.

These are

GRID NUMBERS

– just like on a street directory.

FIND THE LETTERS AND NUMBERS ON THE GRID TO SOLVE THE PUZZLE.

See if you can find these things in the drawing opposite. → → ↘ ↘ ↘ ↘ ↘ ↘

★ STUPID KATT
A1/A2/B1

❏ UGLY KATT
A1/A2/B1

★ UGLY, STUPID
KATT A1/A2/B1

❏ CLEVER, FUNNY
AND HANDSOME
RATT* B2

How hard is this?

Turn the page and you will find the first of our

GRID PICTURES !!!

Next to each big picture there are lots of

CLUES.

* That's ME!

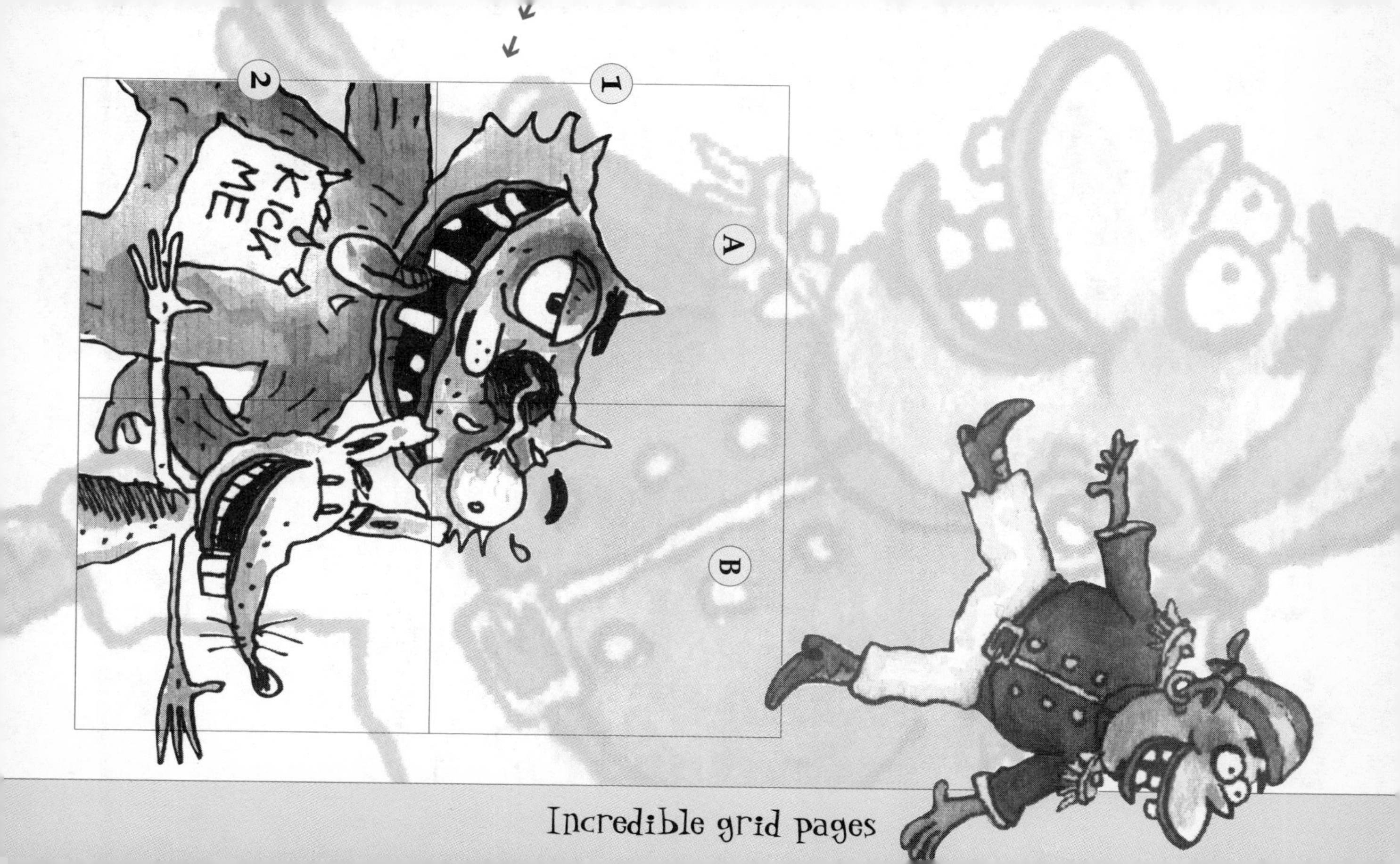
A
B
1
2
KICK
ME

Resorting to the Ridiculous

Hairy riddles to scratch on

- ❏ What is a fortune teller's favourite song? B2
- ❏ What do you call a sultana on a bald head? A3
- ❏ Why won't swimmers have a dog? C2/D2
- ❏ Where do sows run fastest? C2
- ❏ How did the elf get his car across the water? C1/D1
- ❏ Why was the sailor lonely? B2/C2/B3/C3
- ❏ Why do umpires keep a mirror on the wall? A2
- ❏ Why do funeral directors run slowly? B1/CI
- ❏ What do you use to push a doorbell? C4
- ❏ Why don't you laugh at a runny nose? B2

Picture riddles

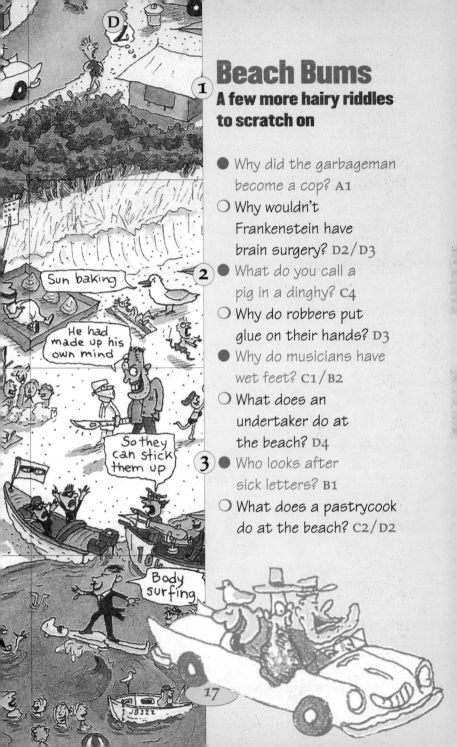

Beach Bums
A few more hairy riddles to scratch on

- Why did the garbageman become a cop? A1
- Why wouldn't Frankenstein have brain surgery? D2/D3
- What do you call a pig in a dinghy? C4
- Why do robbers put glue on their hands? D3
- Why do musicians have wet feet? C1/B2
- What does an undertaker do at the beach? D4
- Who looks after sick letters? B1
- What does a pastrycook do at the beach? C2/D2

Rocks in Your Head!

Get your just deserts with these jokes

◆ Which monster plays tricks? **D1/D2**

◆ What do you call a cowboy who acts the goat? **B2**

◆ Why didn't the koala wear shoes? **A2**

◆ What do you sing on a snowman's birthday? **C3**

◆ What do koalas wear on their feet? **A1**

◆ What kind of treats do lambs like? **B3**

◆ Which parts of a car are dishonest? **A2/A3**

◆ Which is the flattest bird? **B3**

◆ What does a battery do for exercise? **C4**

A few more riddles!

Just keep on laughing

Q: WHAT ARE THE CLEANEST TV SHOWS?

A: SOAPIES.

HEE HEE

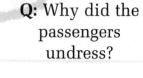

Q: Why did the passengers undress?

A: The porter said, 'All change, please.'

Q: Why didn't the monster have to pay for his phone call?

A: It was a troll-free call.

Q: Which cowboy lent money?

A: The Loan Ranger.

HONEST GEORGE'S USED HORSES

NOW I'M BROKE!

Q: Why did the tennis player need new teeth?

A: She lost the first set.

Q: WHAT WILL THE LAWYER DO IF HIS WIFE PUSHES HIM DOWN THE TOILET?

A: SEWER.

Q: WHY WON'T OYSTERS SHARE?

A: THEY ARE SHELLFISH.

Q: What weapon was invented by a goldfish?

A: The fish tank.

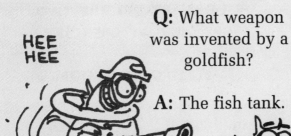

Q: WHAT DO YOU CALL TWINS ON A CASINO ROOF?

A: TWO UP.

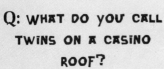

Q: WHAT DID THE TWO SPEEDING WITCHES SAY?

A: BROOM BROOM.

Q: Which is the smelliest ball game?

A: Ping-pong.

SPLATT!

Q: WHAT KEEPS ELVIS COOL?

A: HIS FANS.

Q: Which aircraft needs a deodorant?

A: A smelly copter.

Katt was working on a stall at the school fete when his teacher, Miss Key, arrived.

'Can I help you, Kiss Me?' Katt said.

It was so embarrassing.

He said, 'Kiss Me' instead of 'Miss Key'.

He didn't want to say it. It was his mouth's fault. It just slipped out.

Katt got the **SOUNDS** at the start of the words mixed up.

Is your foot still in your mouth?

Are you sure this clown is a pirate,?

Well he signed on with the rest of the crew, Katty!

It can happen to anyone.

BUT NOW

Katt can't stop doing it.
He tries to say *catch a hat*
but it always comes out as
hatch a cat.

Smelly back becomes
belly smack.

Catch a snake turns into
snatch a cake.

Sometimes he comes out
with really wacky ones.

Socks on feet turns
into *fox on seat*.

These are all just slips of
the tongue. Or are they?

When we make this sort
of slip-up, it's called a
spoonerism.*

It's pretty crazy stuff,
and there are lots of them
on the next six grid pages.

*FIND OUT MORE
ABOUT SPOONERISMS
AND OTHER STUFF ON MY
PAGES (132-133)
FREDDIE THE FLEA

Barking Mad
Untangle these word knots -or not!

- ✗ Catch a hat D3
- ✗ Bee on the peak C1
- ✗ Nicked his pose B4
- ✗ Five for the dish C3
- ✗ Smelly back D2
- ✗ Shake a tower A2
- ✗ Kittens on a mat A4/B 4
- ✗ Snatch a cake D1/D2
- ✗ Boating fleas C2/D2
- ✗ A brat in a bar C4
- ✗ Socks on feet D1
- ✗ Case of rats C2/B2/B3/A3

YOURS?

Spoonerisms

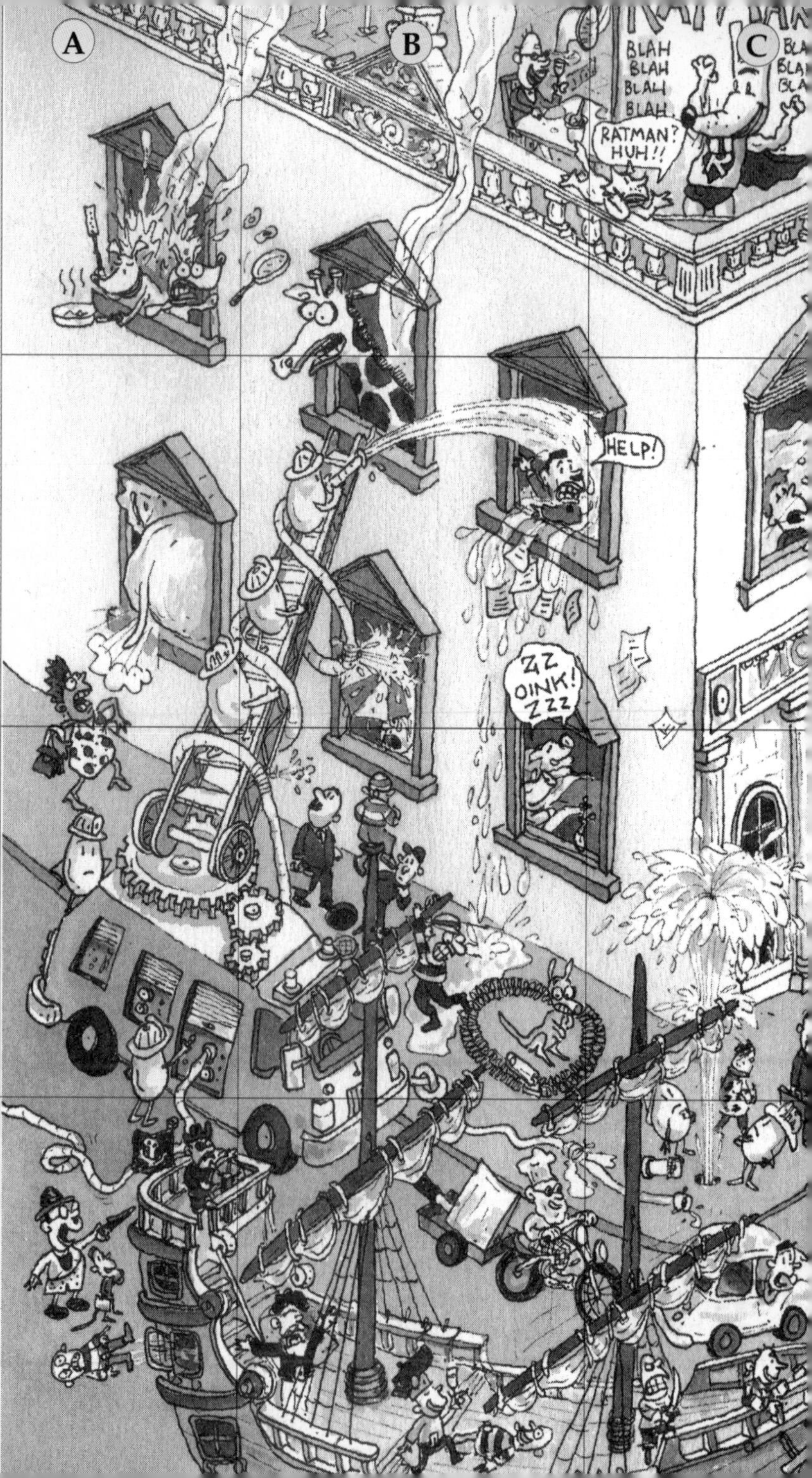
A
B
C
BLAH
BLAH
BLAH
BLAH
RATMAN? HUH!!
HELP!
ZZ OINK! ZZZ

Elephant arrested. Body found in trunk!

- ✔ Frogs are dying A1
- ✔ Rip around the zoo B3
- ✔ Shot in the dark D4
- ✔ Legs on adders B2/A3
- ✔ Flagon dry D2
- ✔ Chook with a copper B4
- ✔ Grown man D3/D4
- ✔ Weeping lizard D1
- ✔ Dogs are hosing B2/B3
- ✔ Germ in a whale D1
- ✔ Fly old socks D3
- ✔ Fat man's race C1

Help
unscramble this messy mind

★ Trace the rain
  A2/B2/C1
★ Coat with a girl B4
★ Walking tall C2
★ Fair on hire A4
★ Lice on the moose
  C1/C2/D2
★ Bat fares C3
★ Slipping on the soap
  D3/D4
★ Wrecked pier B3
★ Rain on the trails
  A2/B2
★ Shoe on the paw C4
★ Not out of the
  snows B2

Spoonerisms

I'm all spooned out!

Q: WHAT DO YOU GET IF YOU STRETCH A ROCK GROUP?

A: AN ELASTIC BAND.

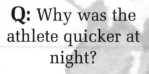

Q: Why was the athlete quicker at night?

A: She was fast asleep.

34

Q: What do bananas wear on their feet?

A: Slippers.

Q: WHAT DO YOU USE TO SHOOT A POP-STAR?

A: A POP GUN.

Q: Why did the witches stop work?

A: They needed a spell.

Q: What book featured a smelly toad?

A: Wind in the pillows.

Q: Why don't cows forget?

A: They have long mammaries.

Q: What do you call it when a baby wees on the street directory?

A: A wet mappy.

OH NO!

Look out! PUNS ahead

It's trade-in time for these dudes!

It sounds punny to me!

Katt and Ratt are visiting Ratt's sculpture exhibition at the Art Gallery. They are arguing as usual.

'You call yourself an artist, Ratt. What's this one meant to be? It looks like a big log of wood with a cat's head on it.'

'That's a **Katt**alogue. It's a visual pun. A joke, Katt.'

'Well, it's not very funny. What about this one, Ratt? A horribly mangled cat. What's this meant to be?'

'That's one of my favourites, Katt.

It's called **Katt**egory.'

'Well, it's not very funny either. And what's that stupid bit of sculpture over there, Ratt?'

'I call it **Katt**apult, Katt. It's an interactive sculpture.

Just step into this seat.
I'll release this catch.
And bye-bye Katt.'

If you want to try more
of these visual puns,* turn
the page and have a go.

And if you happen to
find where Katt landed,
I don't want to know!

* MORE ABOUT
PUNS ON PAGES
132-133

FREDDIE THE FLEA

Ratty,
have we seen
this
character
before?

Page 27,
perhaps?

Bird Opera at House

Otto speaks out!
'Dog paddling sensation'

- ★ Crabby teacher **B2/C2**
- ★ Pat on the back **B2/B3**
- ★ Catching a cab **D1/D2**
- ★ Hairy chest **C2**
- ★ Bed-ridden **A2/B2**
- ★ Dog paddle **C3/D3/D4**
- ★ Grey nurse shark **A2**
- ★ Foxgloves **B3**
- ★ Pig pen **C2**
- ★ Marriage of convenience **A3/B3**
- ★ Letterbox **B2/C2**
- ★ Forklift **C4**
- ★ Tree surgeons **B1/B2**
- ★ Spring cleaning **B1**
- ★ Crane on nest **A1/A2**
- ★ Deodorant **C1**
- ★ Computer mouse **B1**
- ★ Frozen stiff **C1/D1**
- ★ Tongue-tied **B1**

Puzzling puns

Puzzling puns

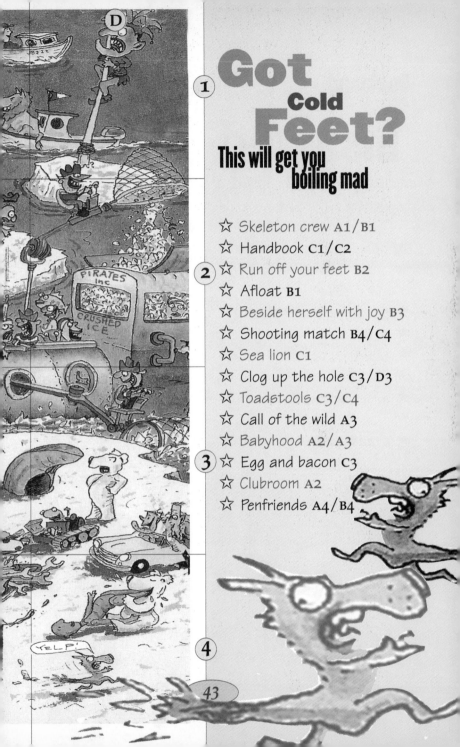

Got Cold Feet?

This will get you boiling mad

☆ Skeleton crew A1/B1
☆ Handbook C1/C2
☆ Run off your feet B2
☆ Afloat B1
☆ Beside herself with joy B3
☆ Shooting match B4/C4
☆ Sea lion C1
☆ Clog up the hole C3/D3
☆ Toadstools C3/C4
☆ Call of the wild A3
☆ Babyhood A2/A3
☆ Egg and bacon C3
☆ Clubroom A2
☆ Penfriends A4/B4

43

Dockland

Disaster!

Pointless puzzles and a pirate's parrot

44

Puzzling puns

Puzzling puns

Smalltown Shambles!

Jokers go berserk
Chaos in Main Street
Reader to the rescue

☆ Dining car C2
☆ Mouth-watering C1/D1
☆ Battery charge D3
☆ Weeping willow A1
☆ Toast of the Town D2/D3
☆ Kitty Litter A2/A3
☆ Nose-picking B1/C1
☆ Defence B1/C1/B2/C2
☆ Riding High B2/C2
☆ Tree house
  A1/B1/A2/B2
☆ Bear fruit C1
☆ Car sick A3/B3
☆ Glass tanks B1/C1
☆ Give him his head B2
☆ Fish bowl A4/B3/B4

What's the difference between a joke and a riddle, Ratty?

Q: Why did the judge say 'No'?

A: It was a short sentence.

A few more riddles . . .

Q: WHICH BIRD CAN LIFT A BUILDING?

A: A CRANE.

HELP! HELP!

BLEAGH!

BLORT!!

Q: What did the two seasick dogs say?

A: Rough rough.

Q: WHY WOULDN'T THE DRIVER DELIVER FISH FINGERS?

A: HE DROVE A TOE-TRUCK.

Q: Why do surfies avoid the kitchen?

A: Because of the microwaves.

Q: WHAT GROWS iF YOU PLANT YOUR HAND?

A: A PALM TREE.

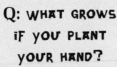

Q: What game do you play on a wet billiards-table?

A: Pool.

Q: WHY ARE THIN PEOPLE FATTER IN THE MORNING?

A: BECAUSE THEY ARE WIDE AWAKE.

Q: What do you call a bikie with a sultana on his head?

A: Hair raisin.

Ratty, have we seen this character before?

He looks a bit like Paul Jennings to me, Katty

Q: What car can touch its toes?

A: A Mercedes Benz.

Q: Why did the chicken keep the phone on her head?

A: She didn't want anyone to ring her neck.

What's the difference between a Ratt and a Spitting Rat, Katty?

The Spitting Rat

a story by
Paul Jennings

ONE

'What's a zuff?' I said to Mum.

'No such thing,' she answered. She took the letter from my hand and read it.

Dear Anthony,

I hope you like the Spitting Rat. Take it to the zough and it will bring you good luck. But whatever you doo, don't tutch it.

Love and Happy Birthday,
Uncle Bill

Mum looked hard at the word *zough* and frowned. 'Bill can't spell for nuts,' she said. 'I think he meant *tough* or maybe *rough*.'

'That doesn't make sense,' I said.

'Bill never makes sense,' said Mum. 'Fancy giving you a dead rat for your birthday.'

The rat stood there stiff and still inside a little glass dome. Its mouth was open in a sort of a snarl.

'It's cute,' I said. 'Uncle Bill always gives me great presents.'

Mum gave a snort. 'Bill's up in Darwin getting into all sorts of foolishness. He knows we're dead broke. And what does he give you? Shoes? Books? A new school uniform? Something useful? Not on your Nelly. He gives you a stuffed rat, for heaven's sake.'

'I like him,' I said.

'I like him too,' said Mum. 'But I'm glad he's in Darwin and we're down here in Melbourne. Fancy giving you a dead rat. He probably got it for nothing.'

I could understand why Mum wanted me

to have clothes for my birthday. Life was tough for her. She had been working hard. Too hard. She needed a holiday and I was trying to arrange it.

All I had to do was get three thousand dollars for the two of us to go to Surfers Paradise. I had been saving for two weeks and already had one dollar fifty. Only two thousand, nine hundred and ninety-eight dollars fifty to go.

When Uncle Bill made it big he was going to send us money. But at the moment he was broke too. Sometimes Mum called her brother 'Silly Billy'. But I liked him a lot. He was always having adventures.

I read the letter again. 'The Spitting Rat brings good luck if you take it to a zough,' I said.

'I wouldn't get your hopes up, Anthony,' said Mum.

'I'll test it out,' I said. 'Maybe the luck works without a zough – whatever that is.' I went over to the cupboard and fetched a pair of dice from a game of Ludo. Then I shook them up and threw them on the table.

'Two sixes,' I yelled.

'A fluke,' said Mum with a laugh. She walked out of the kitchen, shaking her head and not even waiting to see what happened.

I threw the dice again and stared. I couldn't believe it. Another two sixes.

The stuffed rat glared out from its glass cage. Was it bringing me luck? I threw the dice once more. They both rolled off the edge of the table and under the sideboard that Uncle Bill gave me last year. I couldn't see if they had thrown up sixes or not. I lay down on my stomach and peered into the dusty space where the dice had stopped. There was something there. A piece of paper sticking out of my cupboard.

I reached under and pulled the dice and the paper out. It wasn't just any old piece of paper. It was a fifty-dollar note.

'Wow,' I screamed. 'Bonus. What luck.'

Just for fun I threw the dice again. Two sixes. Yes, yes, yes. The rat was a lucky rat, that was for sure.

I showed Mum the money. 'If the Spitting Rat had not arrived we would never have found this fifty dollars,' I said.

'It brings luck. Now we only have to find another two thousand, nine hundred and forty-eight dollars fifty and we can have that holiday up north in the sun.'

Mum gave me a kindly smile. 'It's a lovely thing you are doing, Anthony,' she said. 'But three thousand dollars is too much for a boy to save all on his own. I'd be just as happy if you did the washing-up now and then.'

Poor Mum. Fancy thinking that me doing the washing-up was going to make her happy. No – I had to get the three thousand dollars. Then she could relax next to a pool in Surfers Paradise. And neither of us would have to do the washing-up.

I sat down and wrote a letter back to Uncle Bill.

Dear Uncle Bill,

Thanks for the Spitting Rat. It is grate. By the way, what's a zough? I am going in a speling competition today. The prize is a free trip to Surfers Paradice. If I win I am going to take Mum. She needs a rest.

Lots of love,
Anthony

The spelling competition was on that very day. At five o'clock in the Town Hall.

'I'm pretty good at spelling,' I said to Mum. 'I might win the competition.'

Mum read my letter and smiled. 'You're so much like Bill,' she said with a smile.

I could see she didn't think much of my chances. I don't know why. I was a good speller. Still, I had to have a fall-back plan. An idea started to form in my mind. Yes. It was a good idea. I would use money to make money. Invest it wisely.

I put the fifty dollars and the dice into my pocket and picked up the rat's dome. 'I'm going out for a while,' I told Mum. 'I'll be back soon.'

THE SPITTING RAT

TWO

We lived on the top floor of the high-rise commission flats. I made my way to the lift and pressed the button for the ground floor. The lift was covered in graffiti and the wall was covered in spit. I hated the look of spit. Yuck.

I stepped out of the lift and made my way to the nearest newsagency. I tucked the rat under my arm and held the glass cage tightly. I wanted to give the rat every chance of passing the good luck on to me.

I put the rat on the counter. 'One five-dollar scratchy please, Mrs Filby,' I said.

Mrs Filby shook her head. 'You have to be over fifteen to buy Lotto tickets, Anthony,' she said.

'It's for Mum,' I said.

It wasn't really a lie. It was for Mum's holiday up north. That's what I told myself anyway.

Mrs Filby wasn't sure but she took the five dollars and gave me the scratch lottery ticket.

I walked over to the playground and sat inside a painted drainpipe with the Spitting

Rat and my scratch ticket.

You had to get three numbers the same to win that amount of money. There were four different panels to scratch away and reveal the amounts of money.

I uncovered the first panel. $10,000, $25, $15, $10,000 and . . . wait for it, wait for it, stay calm. Oh, rats. $10. Jeez, that was close. I almost won ten thousand dollars.

I tried the next group. $100,000, $250,000, $250,000, and, and, and . . . $250,000. Yahoo. I had won. Three lots of two hundred and fifty thousand dollars. Awesome. Magic. My heart was pumping like crazy.

Hang on, hang on. Oh no. One of them was twenty five thousand not two hundred and fifty thousand. I felt like someone who was on the end of the queue just as McDonald's closed for the day.

No hamburger. Nothing.

I quickly uncovered the third panel. No luck. Rats.

One last window to go. Scratch, scratch, scratch. I did them all quickly without really looking. And then I saw it. Oh yes. Three lots of three thousand dollars. There was no mistake. I blinked and blinked and pinched myself. I had won three thousand dollars.

The Spitting Rat was the lucky rat. That was for sure. I jumped up and banged my head on the top of the concrete pipe.

'Ow, wow, arghoo.' It hurt like crazy. I fell down backwards and smashed into the glass dome of the Spitting Rat. And broke it. It just smashed to pieces leaving the rat standing in the not so fresh air.

What had I done? Would the rat still bring luck? Would it get mad at me?

'Sorry, Ratty,' I said. 'I'm really sorry.'

I patted the still, stuffed rat on its head. As if to make it feel better.

THREE

That's when it happened. Right when I touched the rat. That's when all my troubles started. I still can't believe that it actually happened, but it did.

The rat took a sharp breath. I heard it quite clearly.

My mouth fell open in surprise.

Yes, the dead rat spat. Right into my mouth.

Oh, yucko. Gross. Foul. Disgusting. I could feel the rat's spit on my tongue. Hot, sizzling, terrible.

I tried to spit it out but I couldn't.

Something took hold of my mouth muscles and I swallowed the rat spit right down into my stomach.

The rat just stood there as if nothing had happened. Silent, stiff and dead as a stone. Its beady eyes stared ahead as if they were made of glass. What am I talking about? They *were* made of glass.

I shook my head in disbelief. Maybe it was a dream. A day-dream. Maybe I had just imagined that the rat spat.

Anyway, it didn't really matter. I still had my Lotto ticket. A three thousand dollar payout was heading my way. And Mum and I were heading for the sunshine. I was stoked. Now it wouldn't matter if I won or lost the spelling competition. I had my three thousand dollars *and* the forty-five dollars change from the fifty.

I picked up the rat and headed back to collect my prize.

As I crossed the street a kid came whizzing past me on a bike. It was Michael Smeds, a boy I knew from school. Suddenly I drew a breath. A sharp little intake of air. My mouth just seemed to have a mind of its own. I didn't want to take that breath. I had no choice.

And I had no choice in what happened next.

I spat.

A little blue bit of spit (yes, blue – and hot) went shooting through the air and hit the front tyre of the bike.

Smeds lost control, started to wobble and crashed into a lamp-post. I went over and helped him up. He wasn't hurt but his front wheel was buckled. And it had a flat tyre.

'You spat at me,' he yelled. 'It made me fall. What did you do that for? I'll get you for that. Just you wait.' He started to wheel his bike along the footpath, heading angrily for home.

'I'm sorry,' I called out. 'I didn't mean to slag at you.'

The whole thing was crazy. Hot, blue spit. I must have caught some terrible disease from the rat. I needed help. But not before I collected my three thousand smackeroos.

I walked onto the Yarra River footbridge and looked down into the brown water. It was so peaceful. A bloke and his girlfriend were just passing under me in a small rowing boat.

Suddenly I took a quick breath. I tried to keep my mouth closed. I gritted my teeth. I breathed in through my nose. But it was no good. I lost the struggle.

Phshst ... A hot, blue gob of spit dropped down towards the boat. *Splot.* It landed right in the middle near the girl's feet.

FOUR

In a flash a little stream of water began to squirt up inside the boat. It grew stronger and bigger. After a few seconds it was like a broken fire hydrant flooding up into the sky. And then, before I could blink, the boat was gone. Sunk. Sent to the bottom of the Yarra.

The two rowers started to swim for the bank. The man looked up angrily at me and yelled out something. They were good swimmers. They looked fit and strong. They looked as if they could tear a thirteen-year-old kid into pieces without much trouble.

I turned and ran for it. I just belted along without knowing where

I was going. Finally I fell panting and exhausted under a bush in the Fitzroy Gardens.

I dumped the Spitting Rat down and tried to gather my thoughts. This was dangerous.

I had spat at a bike and punctured it. I had spat at a boat and sunk it. I never knew when I was going to spit next. It was out of my control.

I had to get away from the rat. Maybe if I put some distance between me and it I would be cured. Maybe its powers wouldn't work at a distance. I shoved the rat under a bush and headed for home.

I was really worried. Even the thought of the winning lottery ticket didn't make any difference. I had to spit when I didn't want to. It was hot and blue and yucky and burned holes into things.

As I walked I started to imagine things. The spit was powerful. What if a robber or a burglar got hold of it? They could escape from jail by blowing a hole. Or put it in a bottle and use it to open a bank safe.

But the spit was powerful stuff. It would probably eat through the bottles. All the crooks in the world would be after me to cough up for them. I would be forced to spit for them day after day. No thanks. No way.

I hurried back to the commission flats and jumped into the lift. I pressed the button for the twentieth floor. The doors banged shut and I started to go up. I was alone in the lift.

The floors whizzed by. Seventeen, then eighteen, then nineteen. Suddenly I took a quick breath. Don't spit. Don't, don't, don't. I put one hand on top of my head and the other under my jaw. I pushed as hard as I could, trying, trying, trying to keep my mouth shut.

My mouth suddenly exploded. I just couldn't stop it. *Kersplot.* A bright-blue bit of spittle sizzled on the floor. Like an egg in a frying-pan it spat and crackled. Suddenly a small hole opened in the lift floor and the spit disappeared.

I could see right down to the bottom of the lift-well. Long cables clanked and clanged. My head started to swim and I felt sick. What if my spit had landed on a cable and eaten through it? I could have fallen to my death.

I was a long way from
the Spitting Rat. It didn't
seem to make any difference.
I was still cursed with its
spiteful, spitting spell.

FIVE

I hurried out of the lift and ran to our flat. Mum wasn't home but I wasn't taking any chances. I banged my bedroom door shut and locked it. I needed time to think. A terrible thought was growing somewhere deep inside and I didn't want to let it out.

I tried to figure it out. The blue spit could eat through anything. And I didn't know when it was going to happen. I couldn't stop spitting no matter how hard I tried.

But. And it was a big but. Would the spit have its terrible powers if I tried it on purpose?

I looked around for something I didn't need. A piece of rock that I used to keep the door open. I placed it on the floor. Then I worked up a bit of spit in my mouth and let fly.

Yes. It settled on the rock and began to fizz, bright and blue. In no time at all the rock had gone altogether. There was just a little blue smear left on the floor.

Suddenly I started to suck in, then – *kersploosh*. Another small blue bomb landed on my spelling book. It started to fizz and disappeared.

I was taken with a spitting frenzy. I spat on everything. My skateboard vanished in a fizzing blue mess. And my photo of Mum. Everything was a target. My bed was riddled with bubbling holes. My desk was drilled right through. The light-shade vanished. My football collapsed with a bang.

POP!

Breathe, spit. Breathe, spit. Breathe, spit.
I couldn't stop myself. I was out of control.

Finally I fell to the floor exhausted. The
spitting spasm had finished.

For now.

SIX

I heard the front door slam. Mum was home.

Mum.

Now the terrible thought managed to surface. I had to face it. What if I spat at Mum? Oh, horrible thought. No, no, no.

I was dangerous. I was a menace to society. Everything I spat at was destroyed. I could kill people.

There was only one thing to do. I had to go away from human beings. Hide deep in the forest. Or find a deserted island. I would never see a person again. I couldn't even have a dog because I might be seized with a spitting fit and accidentally kill it.

Such was the power of the terrible Spitting Rat. A sad and lonely future stretched before me and I was only a kid.

And what about Mum? What would she do without me? She wouldn't have anyone to cook for. No one's bed to make. No one to eat her cakes.

The door-handle suddenly rattled. 'Are you in there, Anthony?' said Mum's voice. 'What are you doing? Playing with that rat, I suppose.'

'I threw it out,' I yelled through the door.

There was a long silence. 'Sometimes I could murder Bill,' said Mum. 'What was he thinking of? Giving you a dead rat for your birthday.'

Her voice trailed off and I could hear her banging around in the kitchen. She always did the washing-up when she was angry. It made her feel better. She was a good mother. I had to get away before I hurt her.

I took out a pencil and started to write a note. My last message to my mum.

Dear Mum,

I love you very much. For the safty of the world I have to go away and be on my own. Do not try to find me or your life will be in danjer. Here is a winning lotery ticket. I want you to have that hollerday up north in the sun.

Your loving son,
Anthony

I folded up my letter and took out the lottery ticket.

I could feel it coming. Sort of building up inside me. Don't let it. Don't, don't, don't. Too late. I snatched a breath and spat. Right on the Lotto ticket. It fizzled for a second and was gone. Disappeared. Totally destroyed.

I hung my head on the drilled-out desk and let a tear run down my nose.

Now Mum would never get to Queensland.

Why had Uncle Bill given me that rat? He had let us down. Put my life in danger. Still and all – he did tell me not to touch the rat. It wasn't really his fault.

Anger started to boil inside me. My life was ruined. My money was gone. All because of ... Not Uncle Bill – no, not him. I wasn't mad at him. It was all the Spitting Rat's fault.

The rage inside me made me think. There was a way I could pay it back. There was a way I could get even. I would get my revenge on the rat.

I ran out of my room and out of the flat before Mum could say a word. Along the corridor to the lift. No way. Down the fire escape – the lift was too risky.

Across the playground. Over the bridge. Up to the bush in the Fitzroy Gardens.

It was time for the rat to get a bit of its own medicine.

SEVEN

I found two sticks and lifted the Spitting Rat out of the bushes by holding one on each side of its neck. I was careful not to touch it.

'Now,' I yelled. 'You've ruined my life. But you're not getting off free.'

I snatched a breath. And spat. Straight at the face of the Spitting Rat. A little blue gob of spit sped at its victim like a bullet.

But the rat was too quick. Without warning it opened its mouth. Fast like a dog snapping at a fly.

Slurp. Swallow. The spit was gone. The rat had taken it back.

Straight away the rat went back to normal. It stood there. Stuffed, still and slightly silly. Just as if nothing had happened.

And I went back to normal too. My mouth felt different. I worked up a bit of moisture and spat on the ground. Normal, clear spit. No spitting and fizzing.

'Okay, Mr Ratty,' I said. 'So I'm cured. But what about my luck? Are you still lucky for me?'

I took out the dice and rolled them. A five and a two.

The luck was gone. No more blue spit and no more money.

I pushed the rat back under the bushes with the sticks and walked sadly home. Now my only hope was to win the spelling competition. Two free tickets to Queensland for the winner. I looked at my watch. I just had time to make it to the Town Hall.

EIGHT

There were hundreds of kids in the Town Hall. We were all sitting at desks that had big spaces between them so that no one could cheat.

'Pick up your pens,' said the Spelling Master.

The hall was filled with the sound of two hundred pens being lifted at the same time.

I crossed my fingers and hoped for luck. I hoped the words would not be too hard.

'The gangster fired a bullet. Spell *bullet*,' said the Spelling Master.

'Easy,' I lied to myself. I wrote each letter carefully. B-u-l-l-i-t.

'I went *through* the door. Spell *through*,' said the Spelling Master.

Oh no. This was a tough one. How did you spell through? T-h-r-e-w? Nah. T-h-r-o-o? No way. I couldn't get it. I just couldn't work it out. My head was spinning. Everything was going wrong. I had another try. I slowly wrote down the letters and stared at them. T-h-r-o-u-g-h. That was it. Yes, *ough* says *oo*. Like in zoo. I scratched my head and wondered.

'Aghh,' I suddenly screamed at the top of my voice. I flung my pencil on the floor and ran out of the door. Everyone stared. They thought I was crazy.

NINE

THREE WEEKS LATER

'Last call for Qantas Flight QF 628 to Brisbane,' said the announcer's voice at the airport. 'This flight closes at 3.50 p.m.'

'Come on,' I said to Mum. 'Let's go.'

We hurried onto the plane. Outside the Melbourne rain was falling softly on the runway. 'Sunshine, here we come,' I said.

Mum headed down towards the back of the plane.

'Not that way,' I said. 'These are First Class tickets.'

We sat down among the business people wearing suits and balancing computer laptops on their knees. The flight attendant brought us fresh orange juice.

Mum was really curious. 'Come on, Anthony,' she said with a smile. 'I know you couldn't have won the spelling competition. You're no better at spelling than Uncle Bill. So where did you get the money?'

I grinned. 'Spitting Rats are extinct,' I said. 'There are none left alive. A man from the zoo gave me three thousand dollars for it. Just the right amount.'

'The zoo?' said Mum. 'Why the zoo?'

I took out the little note pad that they give you in First Class and wrote a word.

'*Zough* rhymes with *zoo*,' I said. 'Like *through*. Uncle Bill wanted me to take the rat to the zoo. He knew it would bring us luck.'

Mum gave the biggest smile ever. She was so happy to be going on a holiday.

'I like Bill,' she said. 'But he's a bit nutty. I'm glad he lives over two thousand k's away.'

The plane started to speed along the runway.

'Yahoo,' I yelled.

'Where are we going, anyway?' Mum

said. 'You can't keep it secret any longer.'

The plane lifted
into the air.

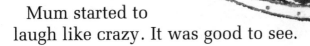

'Brisbane first,'
I said. 'Then on to
Darwin to see Uncle
Bill.'

Mum started to
laugh like crazy. It was good to see.

That rat
could give
us Ratts a
bad name

Q: When is a clock tasty?

A: When time is ripe.

Q: WHY WAS THE BURGLAR CLEAN?

A: HE TOOK A SHOWER.

Q: What shape is an empty birdcage?

A: A polygon.

BLAH
BLAH
BLAH
BLAH
BLAH
BLAH

Q: Why did Jack wear earmuffs?

A: He didn't want to hear the beanstalk.

Q: WHY DID THE TOMATO SAUCE LOSE THE RACE?

A: IT COULDN'T KETCHUP.

Q: HOW DID NOAH CLEAN UP THE ANIMAL DROPPINGS?

A: POO BY POO.

Q: When do dancers stop crying?

A: After the bawl is over.

Q: WHAT DO YOU SAY TO A PUPPY WHEN IT TURNS ONE?

A: YAPPY BIRTHDAY.

Q: What do robbers eat?

A: Takeaway food.

Q: WHY DO BULLS FORGET?

A: THERE'S UDDER THINGS ON THEIR MINDS.

Q: Why wouldn't the bank give the rabbit a loan?

A: It had burrowed enough already.

Ratt, I don't want this job any more

That's OK by me!

'Hey, Katt. You think you
are so smart.'

'I'm the smartest cat you
ever met, Ratt.'

'OK then, what is the
answer to this puzzle?

I'm only one
though make a pair . . .'

'That's easy, Ratt. *A pear.*
A piece of fruit . . .'

'Hang on, Katt . . .'

'I know, I know.
A pair of glasses . . .'

'Katt, I haven't finished
the question yet.

I'm only one
though make a pair,
I help the barber
cut your hair.'

Not on your shirt, but there on YOU!

Ratty,
I've heard
of it
raining
fish, but
pirates?

Could it be
a conundrum,
Katty?

'That's hard, Ratt.
It doesn't make sense.'

'You have to work out
what the question really
means before you can
answer it, Katt.'

'Hmmm . . .

It's still glasses, Ratt. The
barber can't see very well
so she has to look through
the glasses to cut my hair.'

'No, Katt. The right
answer is scissors. The
barber cuts hair with
scissors.'

'Sorry, Ratt. You're wrong!
She needs her glasses to
see the scissors.'

'It's my poem puzzle, Katt.
And I'm telling you the
answer is scissors.'

'It's glasses!!!'
'Scissors!'
'Glasses!'
'Scissors!'
'Glasses!'

Try some of the poem
puzzles on the next few
pages. They're also
known as conundrums.*

* MORE ABOUT
CONUNDRUMS ON
PAGES 132-133
FREDDIE THE FLEA

Conundrums

105

Conundrums

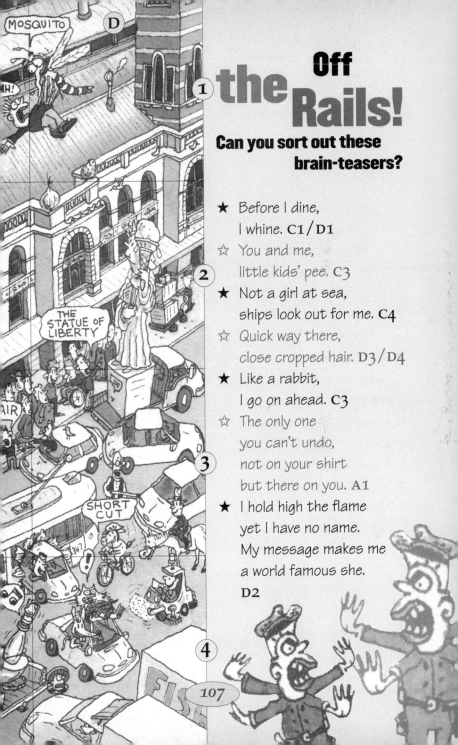

Off the Rails!

Can you sort out these brain-teasers?

★ Before I dine,
   I whine. **C1/D1**

☆ You and me,
   little kids' pee. **C3**

★ Not a girl at sea,
   ships look out for me. **C4**

☆ Quick way there,
   close cropped hair. **D3/D4**

★ Like a rabbit,
   I go on ahead. **C3**

☆ The only one
   you can't undo,
   not on your shirt
   but there on you. **A1**

★ I hold high the flame
   yet I have no name.
   My message makes me
   a world famous she.
   D2

107

Underneath the arches!

Bridge the gap with these cunning puzzlers

☆ I'm only one
though make a pair,
I help the barber
cut your hair. **A2/B2**

★ I can't go on
if I'm weary and flat.
I need some good
fresh air for that. **C3**

☆ Fill us – drink.
Through us – blink. **C1**

★ I help you see,
till your breath
stops me. **B2**

☆ I fit around a finger.
A bell makes me linger.
C2/D2

★ I'm not there
when seas are calm
unless in fear
you raise your arm. **C2**

☆ I'm not in the money myself.
The money's in me
on the shelf. **D1**

★ You write it more
than others do,
but your friends will say
it more than you. **B3**

Conundrums

A
B
C
BARK
PARROT
FART
ARE YOU OK, MURIEL?
TOURS
YES
SKUNK
VISIT LAKE PEDDER 30 m
IT'S BEAUTIFUL
LOOK, YOU BLOKES. CHEESE!!
MOUSETRAP
TURBINE ONE
TURBINE TWO

Kangaroos in the Top Paddock!

Destroy the decorum with these deranged dam ditties

★ I cling to a log.
  I'm the voice of a dog. **B1**

☆ Played by a band.
  Thrown by a hand. **D2**

★ I'm not like most
  of the feline breed,
  I always follow,
  I never lead. **D4**

☆ I have many eyes
  but use only two.
  The rest are for show,
  they are all
  green and blue. **D1**

★ To eat my cheese
  you'd best be fast.
  If not, this meal
  will be your last. **B3**

☆ Stop 'em at the bottom.
  Or people will think
  you stink. **B2**

★ It sometimes talks
  but mostly squawks.
  A1/B1

☆ You're close to a spunk,
  if not a hunk,
  but your pong
  is strong. **C3**

The end is in sight . . .

Q: How do you sack a butcher?

A: Give him the chop.

Q: How did the sick needle feel?

A: So so.

Q: Why did the bus make the footballers walk?

A: It was their coach.

Q: WHAT DO YOU WRITE ON A JIGSAW'S GRAVE?

A: REST IN PIECES.

Q: Why is it good to bet on a beach?

A: It's a shore thing.

Q: WHAT ARE THE FRIENDLIEST SEA CREATURES?

A: CUDDLE FISH.

Q: Why was the prisoner tall?

A: He was doing a long stretch.

Q: HOW DO YOU GET A RED BOTTOM?

A: DYE A REAR.

Q: When do you put glue on a dictionary?

A: When you are stuck for words.

Q: WHAT DO YOU CALL A SANDY BOTTOM?

A: A BEACH BUM.

Q: What did Superman say when he flew off with the scales?

A: Up, up and aweigh!

Q: WHEN DO CHOIRBOYS NEED A BANDAGE?

A: WHEN THEIR VOICES BREAK.

Q: When is a fishing line like a sausage?

A: When it is snagged.

HEE HEE

Q: What happens when you kiss a clock?

A: Your lipstick.

Q: WHERE DO COOKS KEEP THEIR KNICKERS?

A: IN THE PANTRY.

Q: How do mice keep up their pants?

A: With mouse straps.

Q: WHERE DO YOU
SEND A GHOST'S MAIL?

A: THE DEAD LETTER
OFFICE.

Q: Why don't actors like
having a bald head?

A: Because they can't
get a part.

Q: Who is the strongest thief?

A: A shoplifter.

HELP!

Q: WHY IS IT DARK IN A SUIT OF ARMOUR?

A: BECAUSE OF THE KNIGHT INSIDE.

Q: What do you use to make a lazy eye work?

A: A lash.

Q: WHY DO MERMAIDS HAVE RED BOTTOMS?

A: THEY USE SANDPAPER.

Q: Why did the jogger sniff?

A: His nose was running.

Q: How did the baby ruin the soup?

A: She sat on the pot.

Q: Which swimmers are the friendliest?

A: Back strokers.

Q: HOW DO YOU PUNISH A DIRTY FLOOR?

A: WITH WAX.

Q: What did the empty piggy bank say when it fell off the table?

A: I'm broke.

Fried brains

Katt and Ratt have been testing their brainpower and doing a bit of drawing.

'OK, Katt, let's draw a picture of a *Running Shoe*.'

Ratt could have drawn a simple jogger. But instead he drew a shoe with arms and legs, running.

'What did you draw, Katt?'

'It's just a bowl full of food, Ratt. It's not my fault, I was hungry and that's the first thing that came into my mind.'

'OK, Katt, let's try this one. A *Leaking Boat*.'

Ratt could have drawn a boat with a hole in it, but instead he drew a boat having a wee.

'That's funny, Ratt, but mine's funnier.'

'This isn't funny, Katt!
It's just another bowl of
cat food.'

'Sorry, Ratt. I was still
hungry. It does look a bit
like a boat, though.'

'Give me a look at the rest
of your drawings, Katt.'

'Sure, Ratt.'

'What's this one, Katt?
It looks like a whole line
of cat food bowls linked
together.'

'That's a Food Chain,
Ratt.'

'And what's this? It looks
like two cat's bowls
playing tennis.'

'That's a Food Court,
Ratt!'

'Have you done any
drawings that don't have
food in them, Katt?'

'Just this rather sad one,
Ratt.'

Look for the visual puns*
on the next few pages.

* **MORE ABOUT PUNS ON
PAGES 132-133**

FREDDIE THE FLEA

You know,
Ratty, I'm
worried!

Captain Ratt
to you, Katt!

Punny visual puns

Bad Egg Cracks Up!

Scramble your brains and whip yourself into a frenzy

Head on a Plate!

Yours certainly will be after this

- 👁 Bulldozing **A2/A3**
- 👁 Granny knot **C4**
- 👁 Toasting the bride and groom **C3/D3**
- 👁 Fly fishing **C3**
- 👁 Out on a limb **B1/C1**
- 👁 A grazed head **A2**
- 👁 Raising kids **C1/D1**
- 👁 Bolting horses **B2**
- 👁 Mixed up kids **D3/D4**
- 👁 Horse float **C3**
- 👁 Tipping the waiter **A3/A4**
- 👁 Two stroke engine **B3**
- 👁 Head waiter **B4**
- 👁 Lip service **A4**

Punny visual puns

Punny visual puns

A man with three ears!
Where?
Ear, ear and ear

Ratty keeps on and on about some plank or other. What ever can he mean?

I'M FREDDIE THE FLEA

If you want to know how these word games work, you've come to the right place

RIDDLE

a puzzling question

> For example:
> Q. What exercise do cats like?
> A. Puss ups.

SPOONERISM*

swapping around the initial sounds of two words, usually by accident

> For example:
> shake a tower
> becomes
> take a shower

*Named after the Reverend W A Spooner (1844–1930) who made errors like this in his own speech.

PUN

the humorous use of a word to suggest different meanings; a play on words

> For example:
> computer mouse
> It could be a device attached to your computer, or a mouse using a computer.

CONUNDRUM

a riddle where the answer involves a pun or play on words

> For example:
> I cling to a log,
> I'm the voice of a dog.
> Answer: Bark

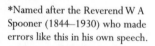

More word games . . .

MALAPROPISM[*]

the accidental use of a word which sounds like the one you intended to use, but which has a different meaning

> For example:
> I went on an exhibition. (expedition)
> Jack was eaten by an allegory. (alligator)
> How embarrassment! (embarrassing)

*Named after Mrs Malaprop, a character in a play written in 1775.

PALINDROME

a word or sentence that reads the same forward or backward

> For example:
> Eve
> Glenelg
> A man, a plan, a canal, Panama.

MONDEGREEN

a series of words, often humorous, that results from mishearing a statement or song lyric

> For example:
> Australians all love ostriches
> For we are young and free
> **instead of**
> Australians all, let us rejoice
> For we are young and free

STINKY PINKIES

a riddle where the answer is two words that rhyme

> For example:
> A smelly finger is a stinky pinky.
> A fat cat is a flabby tabby.
> A glad dad is a happy pappy.

THE END

THERE'S AN ALIEN IN THE CLASSROOM

AND OTHER POEMS

ILLUSTRATED BY
TONY ROSS

GERVASE PHINN

ANDERSEN PRESS

First published in 2010 by
Andersen Press Limited
20 Vauxhall Bridge Road
London SW1V 2SA
www.andersenpress.co.uk

British Library Cataloguing in Publication Data available.

ISBN 978 1 84939 202 0

Printed and bound in Great Britain
by CPI Bookmarque, Croydon CR0 4TD

Contents

Tantrum!

'I'll stamp my feet!
I'll make a fuss!
I'll squeal and screech and shout!
I'll kick my legs!
I'll bang my head!
I'll wave my hands about!
I'll bring the roof down with the noise!
I'll shriek and scream and howl!
I'll cry and yell and bellow and bawl!
I'll wail and whoop and yowl!
I just won't go to school today,
With all the girls and boys,
I want to stay at home instead,
And play with all my toys.'

'Now come along,' his mother said,
'And do not act the fool.
Get out of bed, you sleepy head,
You're headteacher of the school!'

This is the Key

This is the key to the school.
In that school is a classroom,
In that classroom is a desk,
In that desk is a drawer,
In that drawer is a box,
In that box are my sweets
Which Miss Cawthorne confiscated yesterday.

Sweets in the box,
Box in the drawer,
Drawer in the desk,
Desk in the room,
Room in the school.
This is the key to the school.
Decisions! Decisions!

Magician in School

We had a magician in school today.
He did tricks and pulled coloured flowers
                              from a big black hat
And tapped a golden box with a silver wand
And made a white dove disappear.
He picked some children to come out the front
To help him with his magic,
And my friend Peter Gibson was the first.
He asked him what he would say
If he produced a fluffy rabbit from Peter's pocket
And my friend said it would be a miracle
Because he had his ferret in there.

Cuthbert Grey

This is the tale of Cuthbert Grey,
Who liked near railway lines to play.
On the embankment he would lie
And watch the trains go thundering by.
He loved to see the engines gleam
And hear the hissing of the steam.
He loved to hear the clickety-clack
Of train wheels travelling down the track.
Below the bridge he'd stand and stare
At white smoke billowing in the air.
He thought that it was such good fun
Beside the speeding trains to run.
The engine driver shouted: 'Oi!
Get off the tracks, you silly boy!
Can't you read the danger signs:
"Keep away from railway lines"?'

But Cuthbert, he just pulled a face
And all along the track he'd race.
He paid no heed to the driver's warning.
And then one sunny summer morning
Down the embankment Cuthbert leapt
And into the railway tunnel crept.
He thought that it would be a lark
To explore the tunnel, cold and dark.
He never heard the whistle scream,
He never saw the cloud of steam,
He never heard the driver shriek,
He never heard the train wheels screech.
Poor Cuthbert was not seen again.
Sadly he'd caught the London train.
Or perhaps it would be truer to say
That the London train caught Cuthbert Grey.

Downpour

It's:
  Raining,
     raining,
        soaking,
            spattering,
             flowing,
Filling   flooding,
  gutters,   pouring down.
      gushing,
        spluttering,
           forming puddles
             through the
It's: town.
  Making
      all the rooftops oily
        black and shiny,
          wet and stark,
           running rivers
It's: down the windows,
  Raining,   dreary, dismal,
    raining,   cold and dark.
        drenching,
         dousing,
          splashing,
Weeping,   swamping,
  seeping,   pouring down.
      pounding,
        leaping,
          splattering,
            spitting –
              I might drown!

Cat

I am not your fat cat, snoozing-on-the-lap cat,
　　　　　　　　shiny, black as jet.

I am not your lazy, fluffy, softly purring,
　　　　　　　　milky whiskered pet.

I am the killer cat, the night cat, the pouncing,
　　　　　　　　scratch and biter,

The jade-eyed, catch-a-rat cat, a furry feline fighter.

Caged Bird

The canary in the cage,
Beats its yellow wings
Against the bars,
Crying from his prison,
With a high shrill cheep:
'Free me!
Free me!
Free me!'

All Creatures

I just can't seem to help it,
I love creatures – great and small,
But it's ones that others do not like,
I love the best of all.

I like creepy crawly beetles
And shiny black-backed bugs,
Gnats and bats and spiders,
And slimy fat black slugs.

I like chirpy little crickets
And buzzing bumblebees,
Lice and mice and ladybirds,
And tiny jumping fleas.

I like wasps and ants and locusts,
Centipedes and snails,
Moles and voles and earwigs
And rats with long pink tails.

I like giant moths with dusty wings
And maggots fat and white,
Worms and germs and weevils,
And fireflies in the night.

No, I just can't seem to help it,
To me not one's a pest.
It's ones that others do not like,
I seem to love the best.

So it makes it rather difficult,
It's enough to make me cry,
Because my job's in pest control,
And I just couldn't hurt a fly.

Crocodile

Cunning watcher,
River glider,
Old snapper,
Cold-blooded killer,
Odious swimmer,
Devious reptile,
Insatiable predator,
Long jaws,
Eyeballer.

Visitor

The day after they mowed the meadow
Behind our house,
A mouse
Appeared.
It poked its curious black-eyed whiskered face out
From behind the gas fire
And watched us watching television.
It joined us later for tea,
Nibbling the crumbs which fell from the table
Without a by-your-leave
And then returned to the dark warmth
                              behind the gas fire.

Impudent rodent!
I have not the heart to set a trap.

Lizzie's Hamster

When we found Timmy,
Lizzie's hamster,
Curled up in the corner of his cage,
Lifeless and cold,
Our next-door neighbour,
Mrs Gomersall,
Said:
'Are you sure he's dead?
Let me look.
Hamsters sleep deeply when it's winter.'

When she cradled Timmy,
Lizzie's hamster,
In her warm and wrinkled hands,
And stroked his little body,
Our next-door neighbour,
Mrs Gomersall
Said:
'He's not dead!
See him stir.
Your hamster, he was sleeping deeply.'

When we popped Timmy,
Lizzie's hamster,
Back in his cage
Amongst the straw,
Our next-door neighbour,
Mrs Gomersall,
Said:
'All he wanted
Was a little extra love and warmth –
Like all of us, really.'

Scaredy Cat

I belong to no one –
Despite what they think.
Sleek am I and grey,
Soft-furred, jade-eyed,
Pink-tongued and whiskered,
Purring softly, stretching lazily.
Such a domesticated cat, they say.
Stroke me if you will.
Pet me,
Feed me,
But do not try and train me.
I belong to no one.
In this heart of mine
There burns the spirit of a savage blood.

Egg Collector

Thomas liked to collect eggs.
He would frighten off the mother bird
And she would fly high in a fluster of feathers.
Then he would dip his hand into the nest
And steal what lay inside.
He would prick the ends with a pin
And gently blow out the yolk,
And add to his collection:
Sparrow, bullfinch, blue tit, thrush,
Blackbird, linnet, starling, dove,
He had them all in drawers on cotton wool.
One windy day, climbing an ancient tree,
He overbalanced in reaching for the nest
And tumbled from the branch.
Next week at school with broken arm and leg
He hobbled into class,
And through the window I could swear I saw
A flock of warbling birds fly overhead
Rejoicing.

A Really Good Excuse for Not Doing my Homework

I haven't done my homework, Miss,
But I've got a good excuse.
I forgot to close the gate last night
And Rex, our dog, got loose.

I chased him down the high street.
And he ran at such a speed.
But I caught him outside Barclays Bank
And put him on his lead.

Well, I was just returning home
When the bank door opened wide
And this robber he came running out –
He must have been inside.

He grabbed me by the collar
And he pushed me in his car,
He said I was his hostage
But he wouldn't take me far.

I shouted and I shouted
And I kicked him on the shin,
I said I had to get to school
To hand my homework in.

I told him that my teacher
Would be very very mad,
But he just drove away, Miss,
And said, 'Well that's too bad!'

And as for handing in my homework
He said he couldn't give a hoot,
And that if I didn't close my mouth
He'd lock me in the boot.

Two police cars started chasing him
As he headed out of town.
Hee Haw, Hee Haw, the sirens went
But he would not slow down.

At the junction of Victoria Road
Through the window I did leap,
But I left behind my homework
In the car on the back seat.

So, I haven't done my homework, Miss,
But I've got a good excuse.
It all started with the open gate
When Rex, our dog, got loose.

Holiday

We were going on our holidays,
Two weeks in the sun.
Dad locked the door and closed the gate,
And then he turned to Mum.
'Now are you sure we've everything?
Because I can surely bet,
That there's certain to be something,
That I know we will forget.

Have we got:

Travel rugs, beach mats,
Passports, roadmaps,
Parasols, teddy bears,
Picnic hamper, deckchairs,
Buckets, spades, balls and bats,
Hairdrier, sunhats,
Beach towels, sun creams,
Windbreaks, magazines,
Travel pills, toothbrushes,
Swimming trunks, hairbrushes,
Travel guides, face mask,
Surfboard, thermos flask?'

Then up spoke Mum and said to him,
As quiet as a mouse:
'You forgot about the children, dear,
They're still inside the house.'

Letter Home

Dear Mum and Dad

I'm feeling sad.
Oh please can I come home?
I'm in a tent with Martin Brent
And all he does is moan.

Dear Dad and Mum

I'm feeling glum,
Scout camp's such a bore.
I'm in a tent with Martin Brent
And all he does is snore.

Dear Mum and Dad

I'm going mad
I beg you, let me leave.
I'm in a tent with Martin Brent
And all he does is sneeze.

Dear Dad and Mum

I'm feeling numb
I'm frozen to the bone.
I'm in a tent with Martin Brent
And all he does is groan.

Dear Mum and Dad

You'll never guess
It is the worst of shocks.
Poor Martin Brent who was in my tent
Is down with chickenpox.

Dear mum and Dad

I'm feeling sad
As I sit here all alone
In my tent without Martin Brent
Oh please can I come home?

Sunday Outing

Dad lives in Town in a flat
Over a chip shop.
The stairs are dark and damp
And the rooms have dusty corners and faded carpets
And they smell of chips.

Every Sunday afternoon Dad collects me at the gate.
He never comes inside or talks to Mum.
We go to the park or to the cinema
And then back to his flat for tea.
I sit and eat in silence.
I don't know what to say,
Listening to his ever cheerful chatter.
He never mentions Mum.
Sometimes he asks me, 'Are you all right, son?'
And I just nod.

Every Sunday evening Dad drives me home.
Mum never comes to meet me at the gate.
I watch television or I read a book
And then it's time for supper.
I sit and eat in silence.
I don't know what to say,
Listening to her ever cheerful chatter.
She never mentions Dad.
Sometimes she asks me, 'Are you all right, love?'
And I just nod.

Good Parents

They tuck you in, good parents do.
They kiss your cheek and hold you tight.
They fill your world with gentle dreams
And pray you'll have a peaceful night.

For they were tucked in, in their turn
By mums and dads who loved them so,
And by such loving quickly learnt
To love their children as they grow.

Good parents hand such happiness on.
It's endless like the sky above.
So learn this lesson parents do,
And teach your children how to love.

Parents Like You to...

Parents like you to:

Wash your hands,
Blow your nose,
Brush your teeth,
Hang up your clothes.

Eat your greens,
Clean your plate,
Drink your milk,
Stand up straight.

Polish your shoes,
Wipe your feet,
Keep your bedroom
Extra neat.

Straighten your tie,
Comb your hair,
Sit up properly
In your chair.

Parents like you to behave
As they think they did,
When they were your age!

A Father's ABC of Life

Always remember, my son, to:

Act in a manner that you would wish to be treated,
Be considerate and show compassion,
Choose your friends with care,
Don't take yourself too seriously,
Enjoy all that life offers you,
Follow your dreams,
Guard against bitterness and envy,
Harm no one,
Ignore the cynic,
Jog a little each day,
Keep calm in a crisis,
Laugh a lot,
Make the best of what you have got,
Never miss an opportunity to say, 'Thank You',
Open your heart to those you love,
Pay no attention to grumblers,
Question certainties,
Respect the feelings of others,
Stay true to your principles,
Take a few measured risks,
Use your talents wisely,
Value your family,
Work hard,
X-pect a lot of yourself – but not too much,
Yearn not for riches,
Zest for living should be your aim in this world.

Missing Granddad

My gran smells of lavender soap
And has a face full of wrinkles,
And eyes like small black shining beads.
Her hair is like silver thread
And her hands are as soft as a bed of feathers,
And when she's with my mum, she talks a lot.

My gran uses a tea bag three times,
And saves bits of soap in a jar,
And collects old newspapers and plastic bags,
And rubber bands and safety pins.
'Waste not, want not,' she says,
And when I visit, she laughs a lot.

My gran wears thick brown stockings
And slippers with holes in
And a coloured scarf with a little silver brooch.
She keeps a photo of Granddad
On the old brown dresser,
And when she's alone, I think she cries a lot.

I'm Not Crying!

I'm not really crying.
I've got a piece of grit in my eye
Which is making it water.
No, I'm not really crying.
I'm cold, that's why my lip is trembling so,
And why I'm sniffling all the time.
No, I'm not really crying.
I've got asthma.
That's why my breath it comes in gasps
And I just cannot seem to speak.
No, I'm not really crying.
I didn't care when the teacher
Ripped the page from my book
And said my poem was really poor
And that I had no imagination.

The Excuse

No homework, Simpkins?
No, sir.
And what, pray, is the excuse this time?
Well, sir . . .
No don't tell me, Simpkins, let me guess. The dog ate it?
No, sir, we don't have a dog.
Your sister was sick on it?
No, sir, I'm an only child.
You left it on the bus?
No, sir, I come to school on my bike.
Your father made the fire with it?
No, sir, we have gas central heating.
Your granny threw it in the dustbin?
No, sir, my granny's dead, sir.
A monster from outer space took it?
No, sir, there are no such things as aliens.
A ghost spirited it away?
No, sir, I don't believe in the supernatural.
Well, Simpkins, having exhausted all the possible
reasons I can think of for you not handing in your
homework, I shall be most interested to know what
excuse you have?

Yes, sir.
Well?
You didn't set any homework this week, sir.

Games

I hate football.
We have to line up on the field
While the two best players in the school,
Champions of the school team –
Martin Biggadyke and Barry Marshall –
Choose us one by one.
I wait, shivering in my shorts,
Looking clumsy and gangly and cold,
One of the dregs,
The last to be picked.
'Get in goal, Speccy Four Eyes!'
Orders Martin Biggadyke,
Poking me in the chest,
'And don't let any goals in, see,
Or you're dead!'
I stand there between the posts,
Before the net,
Shivering and afraid,
Counting the seconds
And praying for the end of the lesson.

The Display

'This display looks very impressive,'
                              said the school inspector,
'So colourful and bright,
With all the children's work so well presented.'
'Yes,' replied the teacher, preening like a peacock,
'I must say I am very pleased.'
'And he's been in all weekend putting it up
                              specially,' said a pupil.
'Just for the inspector,' added another,
'Because we don't normally have a
                              display on the wall,
Do we, sir?'

39

Mr Fisher's Thoughts on Marking the School Register

Angela Anchovy (she's a shy little girl and no mistake),
Barry Barracuda (gets his teeth into everything he does),
Colin Carp (complains all the time),
Daphne Dover-Sole (thinks she's the only one in the class),
Eric Eel (slippery customer that one),
Felicity Flounder (way out of her depth in class),
Gordon Grayling (likeable but lacklustre),
Harry Haddock (caught him smoking by the bike sheds),
Ian Icefish (a cool customer),
Jeremy John Dory (pushy parents),
Katy Kipper (falls asleep in class),
Leonard Lamprey (latches onto others),
Martin Mullet (just look at his hair),

Yes

Naomi Nurse-Fish (gentle-natured creature),
Oliver Oilfish (another slippery individual),
Priscilla Perch (prickly member of the school),
Quentin Queenfish (thinks he's superior),
Rachel Roach (reliable girl),
Samantha Salmon (that pink lipstick will have to go),
Teresa Trout (old for her age),
Ursula Unicorn-Fish (such a bashful child),
Vincent Viper-Fish (vicious boy),
William Whiting (pale-faced child),
Xavier X-Ray-Fish (eyes in the back of his head),
Yolanda Yellowtail (frightened little girl),
Zeberdee Sander (bottom of the school).

There's an Alien in the Classroom

There's an alien in the classroom, miss,
A thing from outer space,
It's sitting in the teacher's chair
With a smile upon its face.

There's an alien in the classroom, miss,
With the strangest little head,
And fingers thin and bent as twigs
And nails of brightest red.

There's an alien in the classroom, miss,
With long and straggly hair,
And X-ray eyes like shining stars
With a cold, unearthly stare.

There's an alien in the classroom, miss,
An extraterrestrial creature.
What's that – it's not from outer space?
It's just the new headteacher!

Sent to the Headteacher

You again, Farringdon!

Yes, sir.

Can't you stay out of trouble?

I try, sir.

Well, you don't try very hard, do you?

I suppose not, sir.

Three times this week you have been sent to my room.

That's right, sir.

For getting into trouble.

Yes, sir.

You're a nuisance, Farringdon.

Yes, sir.

A teacher's nightmare!

Yes, sir.

A difficult, disruptive, disobedient boy.

Yes, sir.

A naughty, wayward, badly-behaved young man.

Yes, sir.

A trouble, a torment, the bane of my life!

If you say so, sir.

I do Farringdon! I do!

Yes, sir.

And when I leave next week, Farringdon.

Yes, sir?

I shall not be sorry if I never ever see you again!

I see, sir.

Well, what is it this time?

I've brought you a leaving card, sir –
            to wish you good luck in your new job.

Speech Day

Headmaster: And the prize for good attendance
goes to Benjamin Pennington.

(Long pause)

To Benjamin Pennington.

(Another long pause)

Benjamin Pennington. Is he here?

Pupil *(from the back of the hall)*: He's absent, sir.

Lollipop Lady

HERE LIES THE BODY OF MRS PAYNE,

WHO EVERY DAY IN WIND AND RAIN,

WOULD HOLD HER COLOURED LOLLIPOP

AND ON THE ROAD THE CARS WOULD STOP.

NOW IN HEAVEN, WAY UP HIGH,

SHE'S STOPPING TRAFFIC IN THE SKY.

Dr Dodds, the Dentist

Dr Dodds, the dentist,
He really makes me cringe,
With his muffled voice behind his mask
And his enormous metal syringe.

Dr Dodds, the dentist,
He really makes me ill,
With his bright-white coat and latex gloves
And his buzzing little drill.

Dr Dodds, the dentist,
Makes me tremble at the knees,
With his smell of antiseptic
And his: 'Open wider, please.'

I know I should not feel like this,
It is a terrible confession,
Because I'm Dr Dodds' assistant.
Am I in the wrong profession?

A Proposal from Count Dracula

My dearest Count,
Upon my life,
I can't consent
To be your wife.
I do declare,
And tell you true,
That I could never
Marry you!
I'm truly sorry,
But it's plain,
That you, dear Count,
Have loved in vein.

Him Off the Telly

It is you, isn't it?
Him off the telly?
I thought it was.
I said to my friend,
Look, I said, there's that man off the telly,
The one with the hair and the fancy ties.
The comedian,
The one who makes people laugh.
I just knew it was you.
I said to my friend,
I said, it's him all right,
I recognise him,
Him off the telly,
The one with the jokes and the cheeky smile,
The comedian.
The one who makes people laugh.
I'll pop over, I said
And have a word.
No don't, she said.
I am, I said.
I said, he'll be used to people
Pointing him out and going up to him.
It's part of being a celebrity,
Of being on the telly.
Anyway, I just thought I'd have a word.
And tell you –
That *I* don't think you're all that funny.

A Temptation

Apples on the tree.
Juicy, red and good to eat.
Shiny-skinned and sweet.
So ripe and right for picking.
But in the neighbour's garden!

Another Temptation

Fat fish in the lake,
Floats just beneath the surface.
A hungry heron,
Slowly flapping in the sky,
Sees a snack and swoops and dives.

Seasons

Winter:
Runny nose,
Cold red cheeks,
Frosty fingers, tingly toes.
Hot brown face,
Burnt nose,
Summer.

Spring:
Bursting buds,
New green shoots,
Blossom on the trees.
Old brown flowers,
Dead leaves,
Autumn.

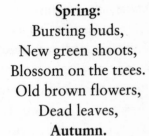

Autumn

I gust and I bluster,
I rage and I rumble,
I shriek and I storm and I soar.
I whistle and waft
And cause the cold draught,
As I breathe on the windows and under the door.

I rattle the branches
And rustle the grass.
I raise up the waves on the shore.
I eddy and whirl,
I twist and I twirl
The carpet of leaves on the ferny forest floor.

Bonfire Night

'Dad, can I light a Sparkler?'

'No, no, and stay right back.'

'Dad, can I light a Catharine Wheel,
A Squib or Jumping Jack?
Dad, can I light a Banger,
A Rocket or Golden Rain?
Dad, can I light a Thunderflash?'

'Be quiet, you are a pain.
I've told you many times before,
Just leave it all to me.
Fireworks are dangerous, son.'

'But Dad – I'm 33!'

50

Fireworks

Flames illuminate the night,
Iridescent blossoms fall to earth,
Red flowers burst into life,
Explosions of glittering teardrops rain down,
Whirling patterns dance across the sky,
Overhead, spinning shapes disperse into the darkness,
Rainbows appear high above,
Kaleidoscopes of dazzling colour,
Shimmering showers of silver.

The Mermaid

'Twas an evening in December,
A night I well remember,
I was drinking in a tavern by the sea,
When I heard a mournful groaning,
A sad and sorry moaning,
'Twas coming from the table next to me.

I turned to face a seaman,
Though he looked more like a demon,
For his eyes were rolling wildly in his head.
He was light as any feather,
With a face as lined as leather,
And trembling lips, a savage shade of red.

'I was captain of a rigger!'
Cried the poor, pathetic figure,
'And what I tell thee, stranger, it be true.
One stormy day out sailing,
I heard a dreadful wailing,
Which carried o'er the ocean deep and blue.

'Twas not the cold wind in the sails,
Nor the cry of humpback whales,
'Twas not the creaking as the vessel pitched and rolled.
For the strange sound in my head,
Which filled my heart with dread,
'Twas like an angel weeping for lost souls.

By the cold sun's eerie light,
I then saw such a sight,
That I never shall forget – and that's no lie.
I near fainted with the shock,
For there upon a rock,
Sat a mermaid 'neath the cold December sky.

In all the places that I've been,
And all the beauty that I've seen,
She was a vision far beyond compare.
Her skin was marble smooth and white,
And her green eyes caught the light,
And lustrous was her soft and silky hair.

Now the salty tales of old,
That the ancient sailors told,
Said that if you look a mermaid in the eye,
You are doomed to spend your life,
With that mermaid as your wife,
And be with her until the day you die.

Oh, I heard the mermaid moan,
Oh, I heard her sigh and groan,
And I knew for sure the creature wanted me.
I could not resist her calling,
And very soon was falling,
Plunging headlong to the cold and friendless sea.

I smelt her weedy breath,
And her fingers cold as death,
As she clutched me in her watery embrace.
She would not let me go,
And she pulled me down below,
And kissed me, oh so gently on the face.

Then she sank beneath the waves,
And I was carried to her caves,
Filled with precious jewels and pearls and gold galore.
But all the treasure of the sea,
Is no earthly good to me,
For I am doomed to stay there evermore.

You think: Why is he here?
Well, stranger, once a year,
I am allowed to come to shore one night,
To warn men such as thee,
Who sail upon the sea,
To avoid this accursed figure's plight.

And now I must away,
For the tide is in the bay,
And I hear so clear the mermaid's distant cry.
Do not think my tale absurd,
But believe me – every word –
And pity such a woeful man as I.

Oh, stranger, heed my warning,
For the day will soon be dawning,
And I must now return beneath the sea.
So, if you're out a-sailing
And hear a strange, enchanting wailing,
Stop your ears, for the mermaid's calling thee.'

Then before I could reply,
The seafarer gave a sigh,
And rolled his eyes and looked at me with dread.
I heard his mournful groaning,
His sad and sorry moaning,
And I saw him shake his old and weary head.

Then without one word more,
The figure shambled for the door,
Trembling in the candle's dying light.
And I was left alone,
Chilled to the very bone,
At the pitiful story I had heard that night.

I called the landlord from the bar.
'Tell me, who was that old tar,
Who sat with me this evening by the fire?'
The landlord answered: 'Who?
Why there was no one there but you.
And you've been talking to yourself for half an hour.'

Dad's Boat

My dad has a boat.
He calls it *Eternal Flame*.
It never goes out!

When I was a Boy

When I was a boy:

My bunk bed was a pirate ship
That sailed the seven seas,
My sheets they were the silvery sails
That fluttered in the breeze.

I'd dream of clashing cutlasses
And the crack, crack, crack of guns
And the boom, boom, boom of the cannons
And the heat of the tropical sun.

I'd dream of far-off oceans
And treasure by the ton,
And mountainous waves
And watery graves
And islands in the sun.

Jolly Roger

When Roger was a little boy
He ran away to sea,
He packed his bag and said, 'I'm off,'
And left just after tea.

'I'm going to be a buccaneer,
Burly, brave and bold,
And sail the oceans wide and wild
In a galleon full of gold.

With the skull and crossbones flying,
And two pistols in my hands,
And a parrot on my shoulder,
I shall sail to distant lands.'

So he fastened on his father's boots,
And donned a coat of red,
A frilly shirt as white as snow,
And a black hat for his head.

He stuck a toy sword through his belt,
And a patch upon his eye,
And said, 'I am now a pirate king!'
And he waved his mum goodbye.

He caught the bus to Bridlington
On a wet and windy day,
And climbed aboard a pleasure boat
That sailed around the bay.

Standing on the slippery deck
He heard the seagulls' cry,
'Yes, this is the life for me, ha-har,
A pirate king, am I.'

The boat had left the harbour
When the sky turned cold and grey,
And the waves began to roll and roll
And the boat began to sway.

It heaved and rocked and trembled
And the sea became so rough
That Roger shouted, 'Let me off.
I've really had enough!

I don't want to be a pirate king,
Sailing the deep blue sea.
I think I'll drive a bus instead,
Yes, that's the life for me.'

Grandmother

My grandmother travelling in Spain,
Fell from a fast-moving train.
She bounced down the track,
And when she climbed back,
Exclaimed: 'Could I do that again?'

My Dog

My dog
Is very old.
He sits in the sunshine
And growls at the world,
All day.

My Son

My son
Is very young.
He runs in the sunshine
And shouts at the world,
All day.

Messy Eater

You're such a messy eater.
Your breakfast's everywhere.
It's up your nose, it's on your clothes,
It's plastered in your hair.

You're such a messy eater.
Your lunch is everywhere.
It's down the wall, it's in the hall,
And you don't seem to care.

You're such a messy eater.
Your dinner's everywhere.
It's on your tie, it's in your eye,
I really do despair.

You're such a messy eater,
Your supper's everywhere.
It's on the floor, behind the door,
It's sticking to the chair.

You're such a messy eater,
It makes me very mad.
For I am just a baby boy,
And you're my grown-up dad!

Haircut

'How do you want it, son?' asks the barber,
                            brandishing his scissors.
'Just a little bit off the top and a little off the
                            sides,' I tell him.
He takes no notice and cuts and chops and
                            clips and snips,
Until my head is like a plucked chicken.

'How do you like it, son?' asks the barber,
                            holding up the mirror.
'Just how I wanted it,' I lie.
He brushes the hair off my collar and smiles,
'Another satisfied customer,' he says.

'You've had your hair cut,' say my friends
                            at school the next day.
'Really?' I say, 'I never knew.'

An Occupational Hazard

Have you heard of:

The Greengrocer who went bananas,
The Diver who flipped,
The Psychologist who's out of his mind,
The Furniture Maker who's off his rocker,
The Plumber who's gone potty,
The Cricketer who's batty,
The Brewer who's barmy,
The Pixie who's away with the fairies,
The Ornithologist who's cuckoo,
The Train spotter who's loco,
The Swimmer who's dippy,
The Arctic Explorer who's up the pole,
The Ghost that is not all there,
The Dog Breeder who's barking,
The Rope Maker who's round the twist,
The Shopper who's off his trolley,
The Debtor who doesn't have the full shilling,
The Biscuit Maker who's crackers,
The Road Sweeper who's daft as a brush,
The Carpenter with a screw loose,
The Baker who's nutty as a fruitcake,
The Executioner who's off his head,
The Milliner who's mad as a hatter,
The Racing driver who's round the bend,
The Baby who's gaga
And the Nudist who's stark staring bonkers?

Icarus

Icarus thought that he would fly
Like a seagull in the sky.
He made some wings with wood and tacks,
And stuck the lot with sealing wax.
Then, climbing to a clifftop high
He launched himself into the sky.
He soared and swooped without a care,
He flapped and fluttered through the air.
Then, on a current he was lifted
And upwards through the clouds he drifted.
He did not think it such good fun
When Icarus felt the fiery sun.
Its burning rays shone on his back,
And melted all the sealing wax.
You should have heard the dreadful yell,
As down to earth poor Icarus fell.
The moral of this tale is clear:
Make sure you have the proper gear
If you go flying way up high,
Like a seagull in the sky,
Or you like Icarus will descend
And come to such a sticky end.

The Plant

Our Science teacher, Mr Grant,
Brought into school the strangest plant.
A curious shrub, so small and squat,
It sprouted from its little pot.

He placed it in the corridor
On a table by the door.
Each day the plant it grew and grew
And flourished all the winter through.

In cold and damp it seemed to thrive,
We wondered how it stayed alive.
And when in summer it was drier
The plant it just grew higher and higher.

The stem was brown like river mud,
The leaves were bright and red as blood,
The tendrils sticky just like glue.
Each day the plant it grew and grew.

Soon it touched the ceiling high,
The plant was reaching to the sky.
Then one cold and frosty day
Our Science teacher was away.

No one knew or could explain
Why he was never seen again.
I must admit I found it weird
When other teachers disappeared.

Then in the library all alone
I found this old and dusty tome.
There was a picture of the shrub
Growing in the jungle mud.

A venomous plant of fearsome height,
Its jaw-like leaves with poisonous bite.
And there it said, 'I'm pleased to say,
That teachers are its favourite prey.'

I placed the book back on the shelf
And thought I'd keep this to myself.

Noises I Like

The crackle of twigs,
The rustle of leaves,
The creaking of branches
In a whispering breeze.

The patter of hailstones,
The splash of the rain,
The whispering wind
And the gurgling drain.

The voices of choirs
Singing out loud,
The giggles of children,
The cheer of the crowd.

The shouts of spectators
When the race has been won,
The boom of the cannon,
The crack of the gun.

The flutter of wings,
The buzz of the bee,
The trill of a thrush
In the sycamore tree.

The hiss of the snake,
The croak of a toad,
The whiz of the traffic
On the busy main road.

The zoom of the aircraft,
In the sky high above.
The sound of a kiss
From the one whom you love.

What Am I?

I have a hood and have a bonnet,
But have no head to put them on it.
I have a horn but cannot butt,
I have a boot but not a foot.
I have a body but cannot walk,
I'm full of gas but cannot talk.
I have a wing but cannot fly,
What sort of creature do you think am I?

The Way I Feel Today

I feel:
On top of the world, said the mountaineer,
Cock-a-hoop, said the poulterer,
Thrilled to bits, said the crime writer,
Over the moon, said the astronaut,
Chipper, said the joiner,
Fabulous, said the mythologist,
Buzzing, said the apiarist,
Buoyant, said the swimmer,
In good spirits, said the medium,
In seventh heaven, said the angel,
As pleased as Punch, said the puppeteer,
On cloud nine, said the pilot,
Beside myself, said the twin,
Jumping for joy, said the hurdler,
Happy as a sand boy, said the holiday-maker,
Tickled to death, said the undertaker,
On a high, said the tightrope walker.
Brill, said the fishmonger,
Grand, said the duchess,
Made up, said the cosmetician,
Fit as a fiddle, said the violinist,
Fine, said the weatherman,
Champion, said the gold medallist.

But I, said the little devil,
        feel as miserable as sin!

Christmas

Chill in the air,
Hoar frost,
Roaring wind,
Ice on the road,
Snow on the roof,
Travellers from afar.
Mother and child,
Angels in the sky,
Starlight.

The Rehearsal

This morning, children, we have a special visitor in school.
He's sitting at the back of the hall.
His name is Mr Leatherboy and he's a school inspector
Come to watch the rehearsal for our Nativity Play.
I am sure he will leave us very much impressed.
I don't think he will be very much impressed
By what you are doing, Malcolm Postlethwaite.
Donkeys don't roll about on the floor making silly noises,
Now do they? They stand up straight and pay attention.
Justine, don't do that with Baby Jesus, dear,
And, Philip, please stop fiddling with the frankincense.
How do you mean you've got your finger stuck in the
                                        hole in the lid?
Well how did you manage to do that?
My goodness, that was a silly thing to do, wasn't it?
Well, if it went in it must come out, wiggle it about a bit.
No, I don't mean your bottom, wiggle your finger about.
He doesn't need your help, thank you very much, Harry.
Yes, I know you are only trying to be helpful.
Just leave the lid alone and put your crown on straight.
Justine, I have asked you not to do that with Baby Jesus,
And, Gavin, will you stop that immediately!
Crooks are for holding sensibly and not for swinging about.
You will have someone's eye out.
Angela dear, I really don't think the Angel of the Lord
Would wipe her nose on her sleeve, now would she?
Use a tissue. Well go and get one from Mrs Tricklebank.
Tyrone, palm trees stand still, they do not wander
                                        about the stage.

Go back and stand on your spot and don't wave
your fronds about.
Justine, I shall not tell you again not to do that
with Baby Jesus.
Jonathan Jones, why are you pulling that silly face?
One day the wind will change and it will stay like that.
Yes, I know you didn't want to be Joseph,
Yes, I know you wanted to be the grumpy Innkeeper,
But there are some things in life many of us don't
want to do
And we just have to grin and bear it and not pull silly faces.
Duane, I did ask you not to wear those red trainers.
Herod wouldn't be wearing shoes which light up and flash,
Now would he? No, you can't wear your wellingtons.
What is it, Justine? Well, I did tell you not to do that
with Baby Jesus.
Put him back in the crib and leave him alone.
I am sure we will fix his head back on before the
performance.
Well, I think we are about ready to start, Mr Leatherboy.
Oh dear, he appears to have gone.

Pantomime

Every year at Christmas time
Dad takes me to the pantomime.
Where raucous children scream and shout
And clap and cheer and jump about.
The noise it drives me quite insane,
And every year it is the same.
When I see Cinders and the Prince
I sit and sulk and scowl and wince.
The Ugly Sisters are inane
And there's nothing funny about the Dame.
I shake my head and moan and groan
And beg that I be taken home.
It's childish, but I have to go
Because my father loves it so.

The Colour of Christmas

Red for Santa's scarlet hood,
Red for the holly berries in the wood,
Red for the Robin's crimson breast,
Red is the colour I love the best.

Red for the wrapping paper bright,
Red for flames in the firelight,
Red for the stocking at the foot of the bed.
It's the colour of Christmas, the colour red.

Christmas Eve

Christmas lights twinkled in the shopping arcade
That Christmas Eve.
Giant plastic Santas smiled
And mud-brown reindeers pranced across the walls.
Tinny voices of taped carol singers filled the air.
People rushed and pushed,
Hurried and scurried,
To buy the last of the presents.

And on the bench before the crib
Sat an old woman in shabby coat
And shapeless woollen hat,
Clutching an empty threadbare bag,
And smiling at the Baby Jesus.

The Different Types of Poem

Acrostic
A poem where the first letter of each line forms the word or sentence relating to the subject of the poem.

Alphabet Poem
Where the alphabet is used as a structure for a 26-line poem.

Ballad
The earliest narrative poem in English is the ballad (from the Latin *Ballare*, 'to dance'). Ballads were anonymously written poems, performed aloud or sung and were passed from generation to generation by word of mouth. They often tell sad or ghostly stories, have pounding rhythms, regular rhyme schemes, fast action and tragic ends.

Calligram
Also called concrete or shape poetry, the words used in a calligram form the shape of the topic described.

Cautionary Verse
A narrative poem which often features a disobedient child or a foolish person who, as a result of his or her actions, comes to a sticky end. It teaches a salutary lesson.

Cinquain

A five-line poem which often describes something in small detail or tells of a simple experience. Its lines follow a particular pattern:

Line 1: The topic (2 syllables)
Line 2: Describes the topic (4 syllables)
Line 3: Expresses some action (6 syllables)
Line 4: Expresses a feeling or makes a statement (8 syllables)
Line 5: Sums up the topic (2 syllables)

Conversation poem

A free verse or rhyming poem in which two characters hold a conversation.

Diamont

A seven-line poem written in the shape of a diamond and which contains a contrast of ideas or descriptions. It follows the pattern:

Line 1: The topic (1 word)
Line 2: Describes the topic (2 words)
Line 3: Expresses some action (3 words)
Line 4: Relates to the topic (4 words)
Line 5: Action words about the opposite of the topic (3 words)
Line 6: Describes the opposite of the topic (2 words)
Line 7: The opposite of the topic (1 words)

Epitaph

A short, often very simply-written poem in memory of someone who has died. You can see epitaphs carved in tombstones in the churchyard.

Free Verse

A poem without rhyme.

Haiku

Traditionally this is a seasonal Japanese poem of three lines of 17 syllables. It follows the pattern:

Line 1: Setting of the scene (5 syllables)
Line 2: Embodies some action (7 syllables)
Line 3: Relates to or reflects the first two lines (5 syllables)

Kenning

An Anglo-Saxon or Norse poem based on a compressed metaphor. For instance describing a kestrel as a 'skys-slicer' or a whale as a 'mountain of the deep'.

Limerick

A short and amusing verse of five lines which follows a fixed pattern:

Line 1: Rhymes with second and fifth lines (8 or 9 syllables)
Line 2: Rhymes with first and fifth lines (8 or 9 syllables)
Line 3: Rhymes with fourth line (5 or 6 syllables)
Line 4: Rhymes with third line (5 or 6 syllables)
Line 5: Rhymes with first and second lines (8 or 9 syllables)

Monologue

A poem or long speech in a drama or in prose in which one person speaks alone.

Parody

A poem which copies the structure of a well-known poem for comic effect.

Quatrain

A four-line verse.

Rhyming Poem

Rhyme is when two words sound alike. Sometimes poems use rhyme to get our attention or to make us listen or to create a pleasing musical effect. Rhyme also gives pattern to the verses in a poem. In most rhyming poems the rhyme appears at the end of the line. In some it occurs in the middle of a line (internal rhyme). Full rhymes occur when the words sound exactly alike (as in 'high' and 'sky'). Near or half-rhymes are when the words sound similar but are not full rhymes (as in 'mine' and 'grime').

Rhythmic Poem

All poems have rhythm, that is, a pattern of beats or sounds. Some poems have a slow and stately rhythm, others a regular sing-song rhythm.

Riddle

A riddle is a word puzzle. Some riddles are of one line, others much longer, some easy to solve and others very difficult.

Tanka

A Japanese verse form composed of five lines of 31 syllables. As with the haiku, traditionally the themes centre on lyrical subjects of nature, love and loss and there is often a quick turn at the end of the poem. It follows a particular pattern:

Line 1: (5 syllables)
Line 2: (7 syllables)
Line 3: (5 syllables)
Line 4: (7 syllables)
Line 5: (7 syllables)